Snail Coloring Book

By Susan Potterfields

ISBN: 10: 153482071X
ISBN-13: 978-1534820715

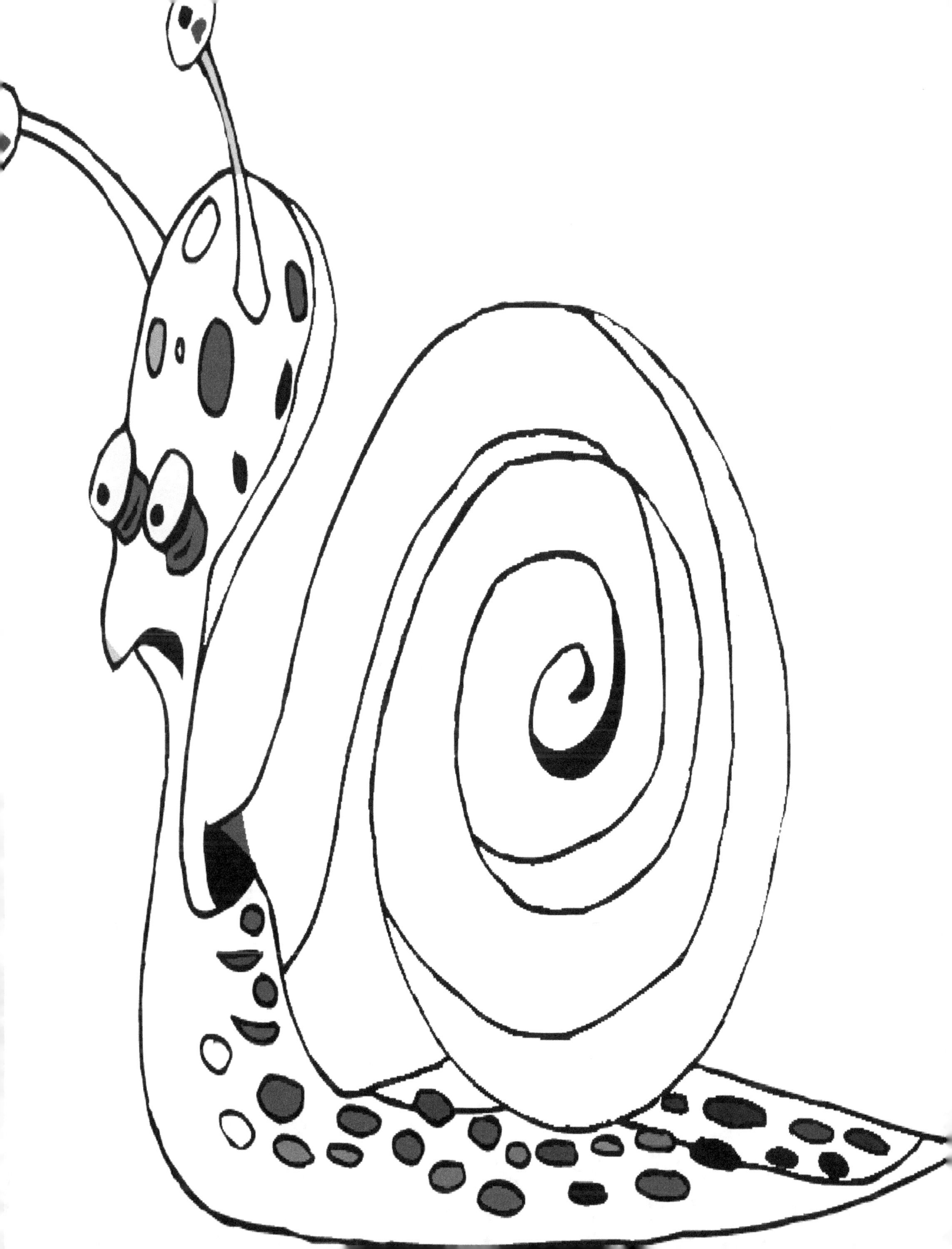

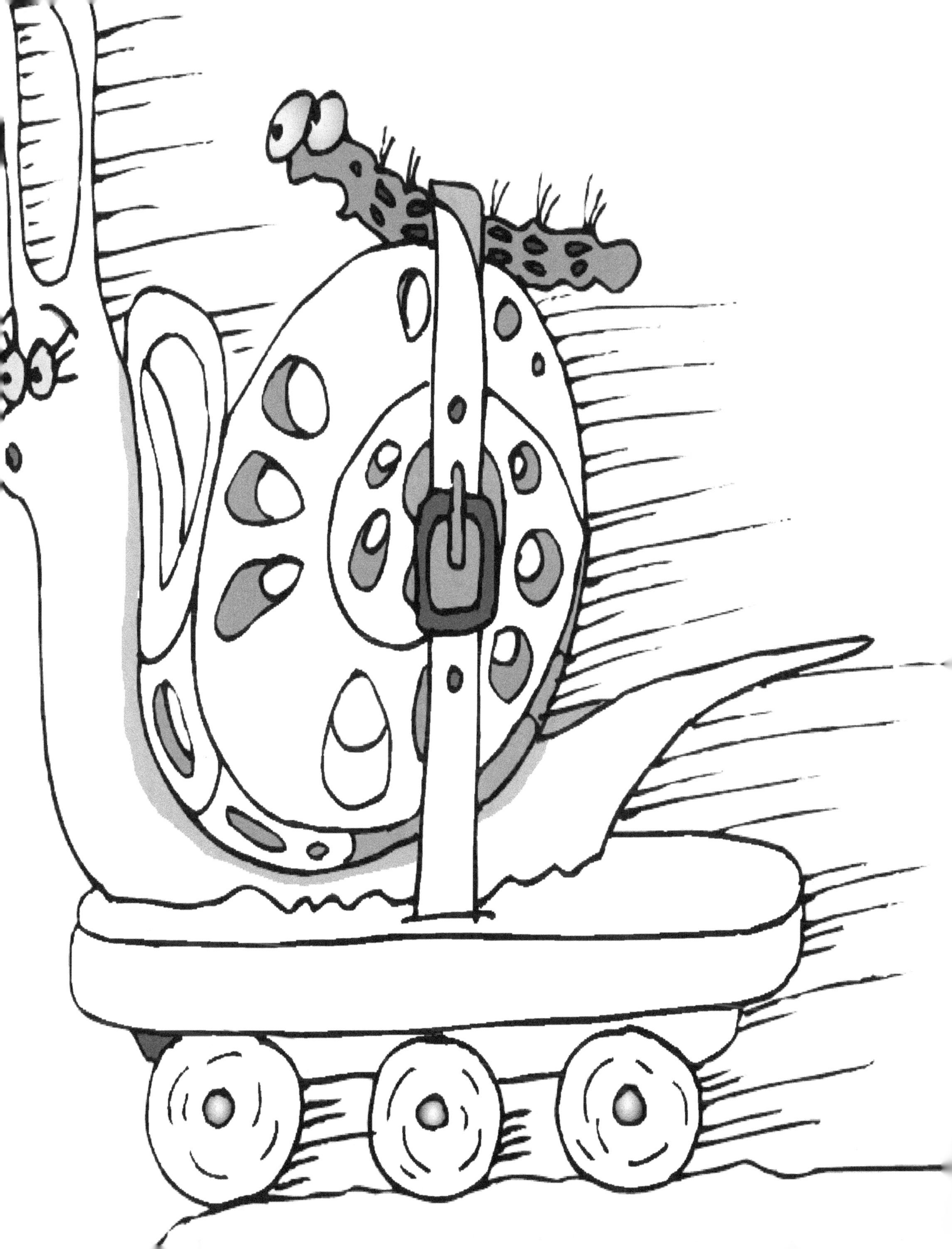

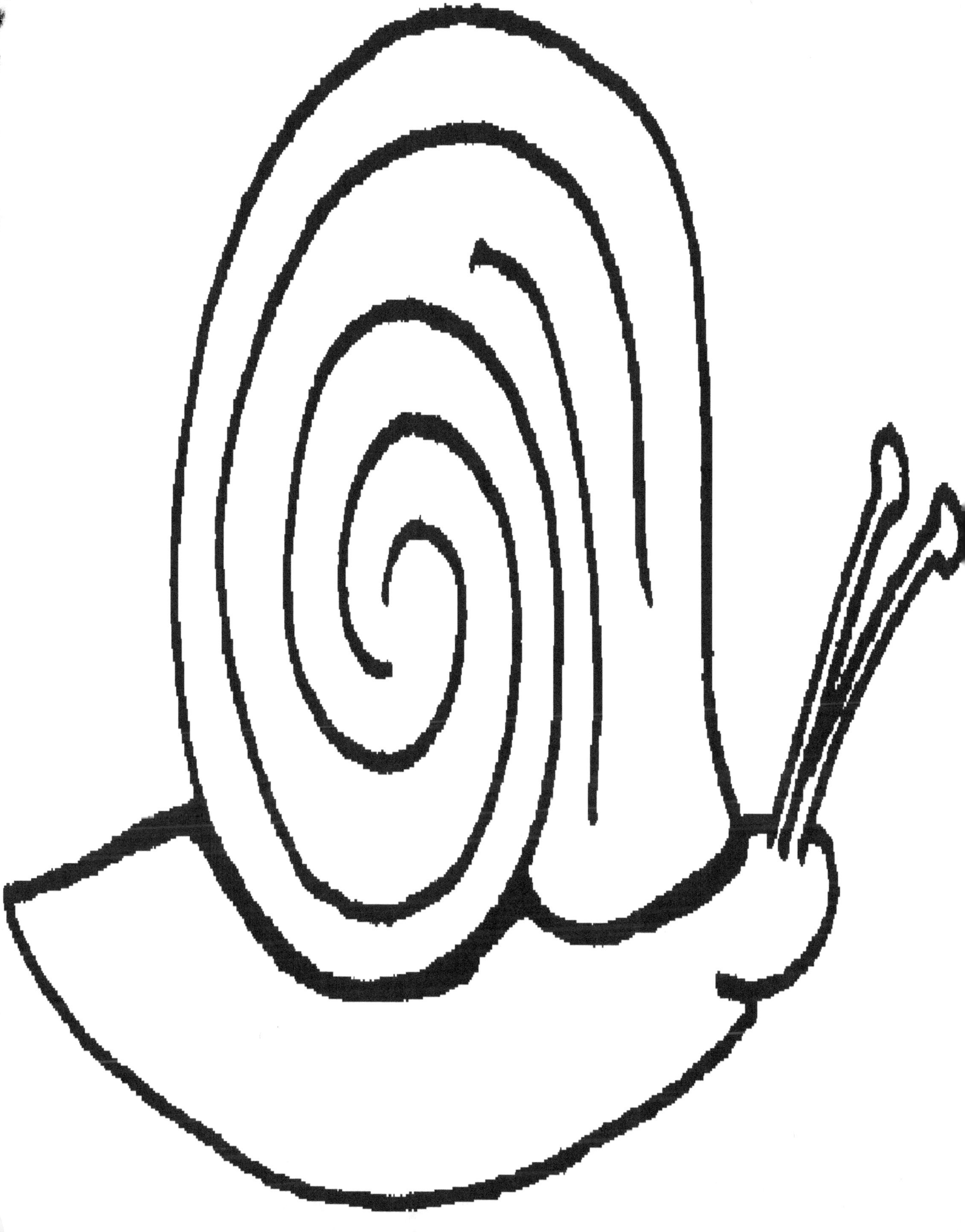

www.ingramcontent.com/pod-product-compliance
Lightning Source LLC
Chambersburg PA
CBHW081142280526
45787CB00007B/3186
* 9 7 8 1 5 3 4 8 2 0 7 1 5 *